The McCandless Mecca

A Pilgrimage to the Magic Bus of the Stampede Trail

KEN ILGUNAS

The
McCandless
Mecca

*A Pilgrimage to the Magic Bus
of the Stampede Trail*

Acorn Abbey

Published 2018 by Acorn Abbey Books
Madison, North Carolina

ISBN 978-1-949450-00-2

Acorn Abbey Books
Madison, North Carolina
acornabbey.com

Cover design by Astrid Jaekel

There is nothing for us but to make it a point of honor to privilege heresy to the last bearable degree on the simple ground that all evolution in thought and conduct must at first appear as heresy and misconduct. In short, though all society is founded on intolerance, all improvement is founded on tolerance.

George Bernard Shaw
Saint Joan

I was about to cross into the wild. After walking for hours on a trail shared by convoys of Jeeps, swarms of ATVs, mammoth mud boggers, and hundreds of hikers, I felt as if I was finally going to escape the noisy world of man and his machine when I stood next to the Teklanika River.

The Teklanika, or "Tek," is a wild, glacier-fed river, infamous for its role in Jon Krakauer's *Into the Wild* (and Sean Penn's movie adaptation of the same name). The story's protagonist, Chris McCandless — a twenty-something romantic who escaped the suburbs to live in an abandoned bus in the Alaskan backcountry — had crossed the Tek in the spring of 1992 in search of anyplace remote and wild. Chris crossed the shallow, half-frozen river with ease, but sixty-seven days later, when he set out to cross the Tek again to return to civilization, the Tek, in the meantime, had become wider and faster and ultimately uncrossable. Trapped in the wild, Chris hiked back to the bus and starved to death a month and a half later.

It has been twenty years since Chris's Alaskan adventure. Over the past two decades, a book has been written, a movie filmed, McCandless has become a posthumous celebrity, and the bus, a popular pilgrimage destination. Yet, the Tek, from what I could tell, hasn't changed at all.

The Tek is one of those borders that separate civilization from wilderness, security from insecurity, cell phone service from no cell phone service. It's that natural boundary where the jungle becomes impenetrable, the desert impassable, the mountains insurmountable; that uncharted part of the ocean where seamen dared not go for fear of the sea monsters that — legend had it — lurked in its depths.

As I stood on the Tek's cobbled bank, contemplating the formidable task ahead of me, taking in the rumbling expanse of a river that has killed and carried away and cut off those who've tried to cross it, whose roaring wavelets were unearthing rocks from the river floor and slicing chunks of chocolaty soil from spruce roots, I wasn't feeling anything close to resolution or firmness of purpose at the prospect of crossing. I just felt stupid for even thinking about it.

The date was June 4, 2011, and it was my goal

to cross the Tek to see the "Magic Bus" of the Stampede Trail.

There was something foolish about my goal—foolish because I wasn't sure exactly why I was about to take such a serious risk to see an old bus from a book and a film that I had merely enjoyed. I read *Into the Wild* as a twenty-one-year old, seven years before. As a young man from the suburban middle class, I sympathized with and thought I understood McCandless. But I was no idolizer or fanatic. The bus, to me, was little more than a glorified tourist attraction. Yet here I am, willing to risk death to see the book's ... *setting*?

I suppose there's nothing unusual about visiting the sites of our favorite books and the homes of our favorite authors. Every September, hundreds of pilgrims promenade through the streets of Bath, England, dressed as their favorite Jane Austen characters to celebrate her works. Oscar Wilde's grave in Paris had been kissed so many times (in reference to his famous line, "A kiss may ruin a human life") that a seven-foot-tall glass wall has been erected around it. The homes of Faulkner, Hemingway, and Sandburg have become tourist attractions. There are *Harry Potter* tours, *Twilight* tours, *Da Vinci Code* tours. There are hundreds of literary pilgrimages and author shrines, but none, to my knowledge, as deadly as the hike to *Into the Wild*'s Magic Bus.

I didn't need anyone to talk sense into me. Risking death to see that bus, I knew, was ridiculous. Would I agree to a round of Russian roulette to tour Flannery O'Connor's birthplace? Would I undergo a series of Herculean tasks to take a dip in Walden Pond? Definitely not, but there was something pulling me toward the bus that would make me abandon all the self-preserving principles of good sense, practicality, and conservatism that I, as of late, had been placing my faith in. I was about to brashly throw out the window the only rational voice from my head's decision-making committee, leaving all the important calls up to a fraternity of my more savage senses: heedless spontaneity, thrill-seeking impulse, boorish bravado, and — worst of all — dim-witted male pride.

But mostly, I was curious. Having already walked half the trail, I wanted to go the rest of the way and get a feel for the place where Chris lived. I wanted to imagine what it was like for him to have slowly died in that bus all by himself. Most of all, I wanted to find out why Chris's story — about an event that happened twenty years ago — is still so relevant today.

And relevant it most definitely is. Even though McCandless would be approaching middle age if he were alive, and even though the book — if it was a person — is old enough to have already gone through puberty and Driver's Ed, and even though the movie has been available on Netflix for years, people still read and hotly debate McCandless's story as if it had all happened yesterday. There are still ongoing discussions about the cause of his death on Internet forums. *Into the Wild* has over a dozen fan-based Facebook pages. The book is always near the top of the charts for Amazon.com's list of best-selling travel biographies and has been, amazingly, the No. 1, 2, and 3 bestsellers (accounting for various editions). A new book, *Back to the Wild*, featuring McCandless' personal photos, came out in 2011, and, in 2014, a book was published by his sister, Carine, called *A Wild Truth*, which gives a brutal, uncensored account of what it was like growing up as a McCandless.

But the most striking testament of McCandless' lasting popularity is the sheer number of people who travel from all corners of the book-reading world to see the bus. There are dog mushing tours to the bus, Jeep and ATV "Into the Wild" tours along the Stampede, even $1,300 helicopters tours — yes helicopter tours! — that land just feet from the bus's door. And people from all over the world, of all ages, are risking their lives to hike to a bus that has become an enduring — though dilapidated — fixture of the national consciousness.

The Stampede Trail has become a passageway on which hikers and hunters, seekers and sportsmen, Speedoed mountain bikers and North Slope militiamen cross paths. The Magic Bus is becoming a national shrine, a holy pilgrim site, a modern-day Mecca.

And I was determined to see it, too. While it's still there.

თავ

Having just graduated from a graduate school in North Carolina, my legs — a pair of cadaverous pasty poles conditioned to the sedentary, I-do-nothing-but-sit-on-my-ass-all-day lifestyle of a student — were in no shape for a hike, even a short, two-day hike. But having just been awakened from their two-year-long torpor and freed from their winter den, they paid no heed to mile lengths or the prospect of difficult terrain; they simply craved movement.

I was relocating to Alaska for the summer to work part-time and write part-time. It was a period of great uncertainty and great risk for me. I had a little under $1,000, a monetarily worthless grad degree in liberal studies, an old falling apart van full of mice in North Carolina, and no real job. I didn't have any "direction" either, except to pursue a farfetched dream to write and publish a book. With my book in mind, I persuaded my old boss at Coldfoot Camp — a truck stop along the Dalton Highway north of the Arctic Circle where

I'd worked years before — to provide me with room and board (in return for a couple of days of unsalaried work) so I could write in the midst of the inspiring Brooks Range. I wasn't sure how hard or how long I'd pursue my dream, but I reasoned that, if I failed, I'd at least get a summer in Alaska out of it.

Because I wasn't expected in Coldfoot just yet, and because it had been, so far, an unusually dry summer (which led me to believe the water level of the Tek would be low and manageable), I thought — in this period of great risk and uncertainty — that there'd be no better way to begin my summer than with a risky, uncertain adventure to a literary mecca and a place I'd always sort of wanted to see.

My friend Josh Spice, who lives in Fairbanks and who I'd worked with years before when we were rangers at the Gates of the Arctic National Park, picked me up at the airport and drove us to his cabin to outfit us with gear. Josh, an avowed "ultralight" backpacker, is the sort of hiker who writes how many ounces his U-Dig-It weighs on his U-Dig-It, who religiously adheres to self-made charts about which one of his sleeping bags to take according to temperature forecasts, and who engages in Socratic dialogues with himself on the great synthetic fill vs. goose down debate. (On a hike with Josh, I once made the mistake of asking him for a sleeping bag recommendation — an innocent, conversation gap-filling question that he confused for an invitation to talk for the next hour about the intricacies of convection heat loss, draft tubes, contoured hoods, and high-loft insulation, which, by the end, had me wondering if he'd at some point switched topics to revolutionary spacecraft innovation or if he was still in fact talking about sleeping bags.)

He looked aghast at my giant pack, which I'd filled with a cumbersome sleeping bag, a one-person tent (that he insisted we didn't need), and a spare set of heavy cotton clothes.

We drove for two hours south to Healy, a sprawling coal and tourist town of about a thousand residents, situated next to the northeastern edge of Denali National Park. Josh parked his Subaru at the head of the Stampede Trail alongside a red station wagon with British Columbia license plates and a Ford Escort with a sheaf of fishing rods and a twenty-four-pack of Pabst inside. After strapping on our packs and devouring the greasy contents of a pre-trip bag of Fritos, we began our seventeen-mile march to the bus, heading west along the Stampede.

The trail, I quickly learned, wasn't the charming woodland path I'd imagined. The Stampede — unkempt, unsightly, and unmaintained — is the Appalachian Trail's trashy, snaggletoothed northern cousin, the sort who brazenly leaves piles of garbage on his front lawn and who doesn't harbor tender feelings for anything except his gun arsenal, which he babies with an eyebrow-raising ardor. Because many locals use motorized vehicles on the trail, as do two guiding companies that conduct Jeep and ATV tours throughout the summer, the Stampede is disfigured with all the typical scars of overuse: meteoric potholes; biotically-barren pale-brown soil that supports no vegetation whatsoever except a defiant Mohawk of grass in the trail's center; deep mud-spattered gouges that tires had etched in tender green tundra where the main trail had gotten too sloppy — all pockmarked with the occasional plastic bag and crumpled can of Bud. Tires had spun over the trail so many times it had become, in some places, a depressed World War One trench that was filled to the brim with murky water into which we had no choice but to icily baptize our feet.

The surrounding scenery, though, was beautiful. It was preposterously beautiful. It was "I-might-weep-tears-of-sublime-joy-if-I-wasn't-being-eaten-alive-by-mosquitoes" beautiful. In front of me was a vast, flat, sunny-green tundra plain dotted with healthy clusters of dark green spruce trees and placid sky-colored ponds. Farther back was the northern extent of the Alaska Range. The mountains, colored a queenly purple by slanting sun rays, were streaked with white veins of winter snow that the spring heat had yet to melt. Behind these mountains were larger, more imposing mountains still entirely and ominously glazed in ice. The sky, most impressive of all, was a polytheistic battleground of gray cumulonimbus citadels—the sort where gods might sling lightning bolts and drum thunder, but would, mercifully, withhold from unleashing onto us the rain torrents that we were sure they were capable of.

After five miles of walking along a mutilated trail but through stunning scenery, we happened upon Ron Sweat, a thickset, red-bearded cook who was resting his feet inches away from a simmering campfire. We asked him what he was doing all alone out there and he responded, without budging an inch, "Livin' the dream, dreamin' about livin'." He told us he lived on the Stampede six days a week, cooking feasts for the Jeep tourists who'd take a break at his camp to eat before turning back to Healy. (Neither the Jeep nor ATV guiding companies go all the way to the bus on account of the Tek and worsened trail conditions ahead.) Ron was keeping track of all the pilgrims he'd seen going out to the bus (thirty-five in the past three weeks including twenty in the last three days, 75 percent of whom made it all the way to the bus).

"How far are you guys headed?" he asked.

It was a question that made me squirm. I felt embarrassed telling an Alaskan — a Healy resident, especially — that I wanted to see the bus, which, at the moment, seemed like a really cliché and uncool thing to want to do. Having lived in Alaska off and on for the past six years, I knew about Alaskans' unsavory opinion of McCandless. So admitting to Ron that I wanted to see the bus was like admitting to a conservative that I was heading to the latest Michael Moore movie.

"We're, uh, going out to the bus," I said. "Have you heard anything about the level of the Tek?"

"It's low," Ron said to our relief. He got his information from a middle-aged hiker who'd just come back from the Tek and who was so out of shape that Ron thought the hiker was going to have a heart attack.

"I'm surprised he even made it this far," Ron said.

"What do you think about all these people going out to see the bus?" Josh asked.

Ron, clearly not wanting to insult us, thought for a moment and said, diplomatically, "I haven't formed an opinion yet."

"But be careful out there," he said. "One guy's been out there for three days and hasn't come back. Looked like he didn't have much food. He had a small backpack like yours." He said this while staring with concern at Josh's tiny, compressed, external-mesh-pocketed pack.

ೲ

State Trooper Jon Williamson has been based in Healy since 2010. He says that there has been an average of two to three search-and-rescue operations per year to rescue hikers who'd gotten into trouble on their trips to the bus. "For a limited geographic area, that's a high number," Williamson told me in a phone interview a year after my hike. "It's an incredible draw on our resources here. I'm unaware of any geographic area in the state that calls for the kind of resources that we devote to that area."

The problem, he says, is that many pilgrims go out there unprepared, often (dangerously) tying themselves to ropes when crossing the Tek, failing to take enough food, and poorly appraising their own strength and outdoorsmanship. In the days following my hike with Josh, I would talk with a lot of the Healy locals, and it seemed like everyone had his or her own anecdote about crazy pilgrims headed to the bus. Rusty Lasell, fire chief of the Tri-Valley Fire Department, says he once spotted two mountain bikers heading to the bus carrying no gear and wearing nothing but Speedos. Jon Nierenberg, who owns the EarthSong Lodge on Stampede Road, and who conducts dog mushing tours to the bus during the winter, told me that a pilgrim returned from the bus "half dead" because the pilgrim had chosen to faithfully emulate Mc-Candless's adventure by taking with him no more food than a bag of rice. In other cases, pilgrims have wandered off the trail and gotten lost. Others get injured or stuck at the Tek. In August 2011, a 53-year-old Tennessee man had to be rescued by helicopter because the Tek had risen when he tried to re-cross it. In May 2013, a group of hikers were rescued by helicopter, followed by another helicopter rescue in June. Tragically, in August 2010, a 29-year-old Swiss woman drowned.

Given that rescues can be quite costly (it's $1,700 just to get the blades on a helicopter turning, Trooper Williamson told me) and that they put rescuers — many of whom are local volunteers — in danger, many of the local townspeople, who generally didn't like McCandless to begin with, have asked that the bus be moved or burned down. Dermot Cole, a columnist for the *Fairbanks Daily News-Miner*, proposed that it be sent to a junkyard or to an amusement park in Fairbanks. Chief Lasell wonders if it would be best to drag the bus out and turn it into an espresso shop.

But there are those who care dearly about the bus. We met two such pilgrims — both tall and slim 24-year-old Frenchmen — in a grassy field of tussocks, where there was no clear trail, but a sprawling selection of muddy tire tracks, the messiest of which we presumed was leading us in the right direction. They had made it to the bus and were headed back to Healy. "Right now, we're dead," said a cheerful Maxime Gouyou Beauchamps, referring to their sluggish gait.

Maxime and his friend Robin had planned their Yukon-Alaska trip ten months before. "We don't have that much land [in France]," said Maxime. "Yukon and Alaska have been dream for many years." They were both exhausted but clearly satisfied with their trip, returning with the warm glow of having spent their time wisely. "It was real world feeling," was all Maxime could say.

It struck me, though, how neither of them were McCandless fanatics. In fact, Maxime hadn't even read the book until he came across a spare copy in the bus. Later, at the Tek, we'd bump into a group of seven more pilgrims coming back from the bus (six males and one female, all in their twenties), and none of them had struck me as people who were particularly moved by McCandless's story, either. It seemed like everyone was going to the bus because, well, everyone was going to the bus. They weren't going so much to receive a spiritual epiphany, or to solemnly press their palms against a sacred object, or to pay homage to the dead. They were going to participate in a cultural event, to snap a photo seated in the iconic McCandless pose for a new Facebook headshot, to do something "cool": things that Josh and I were more or less guilty of. I couldn't help but think about all the injuries and rescues and deaths. People are getting hurt and lost, and taxpayers are paying for the rescues, and for what? For bragging rights? For backpacker cred? Maybe, I thought, as the locals suggest, the bus should be moved. If people aren't getting anything real or profound out of their experiences, then, well, maybe it was reasonable to move the bus so as to discourage future pilgrims from going out there and risking their lives.

∾∾

This was the worst time for me to be having a sobering realization. After stumbling in fields of tussocks, kicking my ankles against mini icebergs the size of shoeboxes bathing in ATV-created canals, and marching over bogs of muck and mud and melted permafrost, we'd made it to the Tek, whose staggering breadth made me feel even more sober-minded. I was sober-squared, and any sense of idealism and optimism and macho-ism had vanished now that I was reminded of my feeble human form in the presence of such a devastating cascade of brute power, which angrily flooded down the valley like fire out of a dragon's throat.

Looking at Josh with wide, concerned eyes,

thinking but not saying, "Sure you want to do this?," I swallowed glumly. We hunted down a pair of walking sticks that someone else had clearly used before us, sat down to nervously overindulge in our stock of Quaker Chewy Granola Bars, and discussed our crossing strategy, which amounted to: Ken go first, Josh videotape disaster.

I stood on the river's edge, pondering the impossible task ahead of me. The Tek brought to mind a stampede of water buffalo, a send-everyone linebacker blitz, a ruthless aerial predator whose nature had not been blessed with the capacity for compassion. It was a dark prophecy that carries the air of indifference and inevitability, with none of the poetry of replenishment and rejuvenation that other, kinder rivers bespeak. Standing next to the Tek is that moment in your dreams when you're trying to run away but your legs are so heavy and wobbly that you can't help but stare your worst fear in the face.

I was amazed that — according to all local reports — the water level of the Tek was actually really low for that time of the summer. Crossing it at its worst, which McCandless had to consider, surely would be suicide, and it was no wonder to me why he turned back to die a less violent death in the bus.

I walked out into the Tek with sideways footsteps, facing upstream, my walking stick in front of me. I wore my backpack straps loose, and I un-buckled my hip belt in case I needed to slip out of my pack if I was knocked over.

It wasn't until I was knee-high in the Tek that I was able to appreciate how cold the water was. The water was unworldly cold—so cold it seemed to have defied physical law and maintained its numbing liquid form despite being well below freezing. I no longer had feet I could feel, just two blocky stumps that I flung in front of the other powered by legs that were still, thankfully, fully operational. I wasn't even halfway across when I felt the first stirrings of panic, which, in due time, would either turn me into an immobile statue of inaction or cause me to make a series of abrupt squirrelish movements that would surely dislodge my feet from the slick, cobbled river floor, finally giving the Tek its opportunity to launch me miles into a watery wilderness out of which I wasn't sure I'd be able to escape.

Reminding myself that this wasn't the time for bravado or pride, I turned back, telling Josh that we ought to find a better place to cross.

After walking about a quarter of a mile along the edge of the Tek, we found a spot where the Tek divided into two branches, both of which we hoped were weaker than the united channel I'd failed to cross. The water, in this first branch, was still gushing violently, but I only needed to go about twenty-five feet before getting to the opposite bank.

I plunged my legs in, advancing confidently toward the opposite bank with slow, deliberate steps. The water, here, was hip-high, just about completely saturating my pants. Halfway across, it felt like I was trying to push against a wall of thick, impenetrable cobwebs. I was losing control. My feet were helplessly being pushed backward in the current, skiing up and down the rocks while I did everything I could to stay upright.

I jammed my staff into the river floor, where it stayed put, giving me a moment to get my feet back into place. I was just a yard from the bank, so I abandoned my stance and leapt to the bank, heartily embracing a hunk of sod before raising my arms triumphantly. Josh, several inches taller than me, and carrying a lighter load, had far less trouble, slicing his legs through the current with his long, strong moose legs.

When he got to the bank, we gave one another enthusiastic handshakes while flashing irrepressible grins. The second branch of the Tek proved far easier, so — with the crossing off our minds — the Alaskan landscape assumed an even prettier, sepia-toned form in the dusky twilight of a summer evening. Overcome with a sense of victory, I felt like unleashing a throaty barbarian roar to the surrounding wild, forest-covered hills.

Goddamn, life is good, I thought and probably said.

Onward to the bus.

ဏၥ

We'd been hiking for nearly eight hours, so our original spirited speed, by now, had slackened into a zombie-ish, boot-dragging shuffle, and our river crossing high had all but mellowed as we haggardly soldiered on to the bus, our clothes now half-saturated with cold river water.

I'd admired, along the way, baby blue butterflies clinging to purple lupine, prowling beavers in their pond kingdoms, and a motionless cow moose with two calves by her flanks warily inspecting us from a copse of birch trees—all of which were slowing reminding me that I was in Alaska and that I'd have the whole summer to savor the simple joys of taking quiet hikes, spotting wildlife, and falling in love again with this land of my dreams, this topography of my soul, this home of my heart: Alaska: big, beautiful, wild.

My reverie was interrupted by a vibration that I felt in the soles of my feet, followed by an ambiguous rumbling in the distance.

"Do you hear that?" I asked Josh, pausing to let the sounds identify themselves.

"Yeah, what is it?"

Suddenly, two bright headlights flashed from the top of the hill, announcing the approach of an elephantine "mud bogger"—a souped-up truck with six headlights, a winch beneath the grill, and humungous four-foot-tall tires. Despite the ever-present tire tracks, spotting a vehicle several miles beyond the Tek, on this trail, at this late hour, still felt uncharacteristic, out of place, downright alien. It might as well have been a UFO blinding us with its blue abduction beam.

To make room for us, the driver turned the wheel and, without scruple, crushed under his tires a stand of hopeful willow saplings. There were two guys in the truck: the driver — a portly, slightly drunk white guy; and his friend — a darker-skinned and silent passenger whose ethnicity and level of intoxication weren't as discernible. Emblazoned on the side of the black truck in white lettering was a logo reading: "North Slope Militia: God, Guns, and Oil."

I couldn't help but project onto him and his truck all the resentment that I'd accumulated over the past six years of living in Alaska. Since 2005, I'd been working at various seasonal jobs across the state. I'd been a backcountry ranger for the National Park Service, a river guide on the Koyukuk River, a cook for ice road truckers, and a dishwasher up in the oil fields. I'd come across men like these guys hundreds of times before — truckers, miners, oil men, hunting guides — whose jobs and hobbies included some element of extraction, pollution, or death. I saw in those mud-caked tires an unquestioned ardor for unfettered, unregulated, wild-west capitalism; I saw a slew of hare-brained, wild-eyed ideologies, starting with their staunch — yet laughably hypocritical — libertarianism; I saw the aerial genocides of wolf packs, the mounted heads of grizzlies, the slaughter of caribou populations; I saw the damming of pristine creeks and mowing down of virgin forests to extract some shiny mineral; I saw the paving of roads to mines and the erecting of bridges to nowhere; I saw a manifest destiny to disfigure and deform this last corner of wild earth into an Ayn Rand wasteland of plunder and profit.

He was actually a nice guy — as they all are — and while I still found something vaguely immoral about his monstrous tires, I reminded myself that I ought to be careful not to misplace my resentments. He told us that he and his friend had gone out to drink some beers by the bus.

"There's something about that bus," he said wistfully. "Something cool."

The conversation meandered to McCandless, and he issued the standard Alaskan line about how McCandless was unprepared, and that, "If you're from up here in Alaska, you know what you're getting into."

This guy wasn't exactly one of them, but he still reminded me of the many Alaskans I'd come across who'd froth moral indignation and deliver holier-than-thou denunciations whenever the subject of McCandless or the bus pilgrims would come up. Take, for example, some responses to the *Fairbanks Daily News-Miner* article about a recent pilgrim rescue story. A commenter with the username, Use_your_head, says, "That friggin bus should be burned to the ground and then covered with dirt." RealAlaskan also wishes to "burn the bus" so that "it quits attracting stupid people." Bogtrotter believes the bus ought to remain because it provides "a service removing idiots from the gene pool." A Healy EMT told me not to glorify this story "Because then the idiots will come out here more." A firefighter, shaking his head in disbelief, added, "I am amazed just how many people think that that thing's a shrine. We think the guy was an idiot."

There is something telling about Alaskans' disgust with McCandless. It's true that, because of McCandless, Alaskans have had to pay for costly rescues (and their disgust, in this regard, seems justifiable), but there's more to their disgust than the mere waste of taxpayer dollars and the annoyance of having to deal with all these so-called idiots. It's a disgust that's too angry, too bitter, *too borderline violent*. There is something about Mc-

Candless's story that challenges the locals' identity, their self-image, their very "Alaskanness."

Despite the popular perception of Alaska as virgin country inhabited by flat-stomached Jeremiah Johnsons who hunt animals on foot and live in sod-roofed log cabins, the real Alaska and the real Alaskan are actually quite ordinary: airport-sized Walmarts, vast grids of suburban sprawl, appalling obesity and all.

They are a people plagued with paradox. Alaskans pride themselves for their independence, yet 93 percent of the labor force hold full-time nine-to-five jobs. They have fierce relationships with nature, yet two-thirds of them live in urban environments. They're expert outdoorsmen and women, yet on most of their outdoor excursions they're straddling some smelly motorized machine. They're anti-government, yet Alaska receives the most federal funding per capita than all other states ($20,351.13 per resident, which is more than twice the national average, according to a 2010 *New York Times* article). They're radically self-sufficient, yet they pay the lowest state and local tax rates in the nation largely because of revenue from the oil industry. And because Alaska has the highest turnover rate, most Alaskans are hardly Alaskan (only 41 percent having actually been born in the state, according to a 2018 report). Born in the state or not, they consider Alaska "their" land, ardently guarding it from the federal government and meddling environmentalists who try to curb the state's exploitative policies. Yet their "possession" of the state and all of its resources is arguable since their family roots in the state run, at the very most, a couple of generations deep (excepting, of course, the Native and Inuit populations, who, as it turns out, do not seem to be at all bothered by the whole McCandless dilemma and aren't incredibly enthusiastic about industrial development).

Into the Wild works as a book because it is, by all standards, a tragedy. McCandless's death was so fraught with symbolism, significance, and — in an abstract sort of way — sacrifice, that it was a work of literature even before Krakauer put it to page. It works as a tragedy because there is great meaning in the protagonist's misfortune, a bright glitter of beauty in the black gloom of death. McCandless, when he went to live in that bus at the age of twenty-four, was the epitome of youthful spontaneity and adventurousness and idealism, almost to the point of allegory. He died before he could go to grad school, before he could get a job, before he could buy a home, marry a pretty wife, remodel his basement, subscribe to *The Wall Street Journal*, and question if his quest for money and things lent his life as much meaning as the adventures he'd lived out as a younger man.

The Stampede Trail

The author on the Stampede Trail

The author walking the Stampede Trail, much of which is under water because of vehicle overuse

Pilgrims from France on the Stampede

Pilgrims crossing the Teklanika River, coming back from the bus

The author crossing the Teklanika River

Local man coming back from the bus in his mud bogger

The Magic Bus

The author first entering the bus

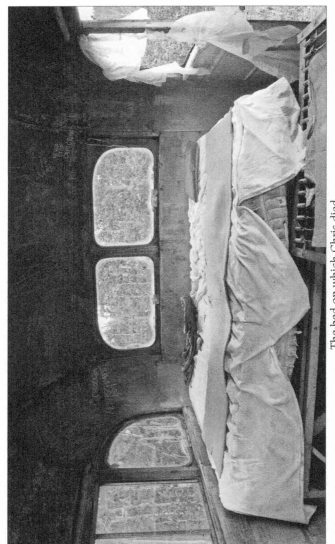

The bed on which Chris died

The front of the bus

The ceiling, etched with names and messages

The author and the bus

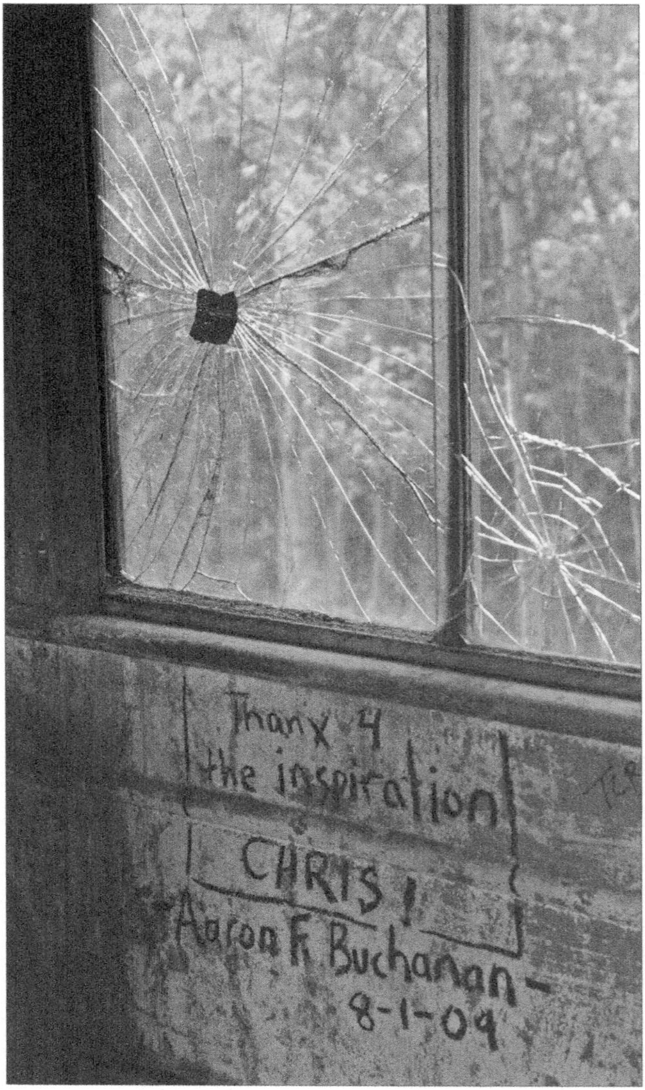
Thanx 4
the inspiration
CHRIS!
Aaron F. Buchanan-
8-1-09

09/16/10

Came all the way from Guadalajara, Mexico, to find this place. Acompanied by my two best friends, like before, like every second in my heart. I pay my respect to Chris, to all his family and everyone who ever managed to get here.

Now I can go on with my life.

José Aguiar de Pablo (1977-?)

Since I saw the Movie I Felt touched by chris's story. Now I am here with my two best friend, and I Feel full of Joy, My wife shares with me this feeling for the story and I dedicate My way back to her!!

Michell Casab

From the bus journal

The photographer and author in standard bus pose

The best tragedies — like *Into the Wild* — are actually quite un-tragic. If Romeo and Juliet hadn't died in the name of love, they surely would have been subjected to the unforeseen unpleasantries of matrimony: pubic hairs left on bars of soap, spiteful toilet lid policy infractions, insufferable in-laws, etc. Instead, they died in a moment of extreme devotion and passion and belief — at the very height of human existence. Because they died before they could fall out of love, their death isn't a tragedy; it's a mercy.

When McCandless died, he, too, died with his idealism. His death was unfortunate — obviously — but it's also a mercy that McCandless wouldn't come back to civilization to be jaded by age, corrupted by money, and bothered by an enlarged prostate. And from his death, a symbol is born. As Romeo and Juliet are to love, Chris McCandless is to absolute freedom, to principled self-reliance, to uncompromised individuality, to chasing your dream with everything you've got, even at the risk of death.

Many people move to Alaska to reinvent themselves in a rugged landscape. Some might live in a dry cabin for a couple of years, but most will end up either leaving the state, seizing a well-paying job opportunity, or buying a home in Fairbanks or Anchorage so they can again savor the comforts and conveniences they'd momentarily done without. There's nothing wrong with any of this, as comfort and security and domesticity seem to be human longings as natural as the desire to leave it all and take to the open road. Yet McCandless's story pricks a sensitive nerve. Alaskans call McCandless stupid and suicidal and feel something close to hatred for him because he went into the wilderness unprepared. But they don't really hate him because of his unpreparedness. (Who could hate anyone for being unprepared?) They hate him, rather, because he lived alone, off the grid, killed his moose, and almost made it out alive. They hate McCandless because his uncompromised nature reminds them of their compromised lives. Because he out-Alaskaned the Alaskans.

∽

After ten hours, two river crossings, and seventeen miles, we finally made it to the bus just before midnight. We'd been anticipating this moment the whole trip, yet — when we finally arrived — it felt as if we'd happened upon it unexpectedly, as if we'd forgotten what we'd originally set out to do.

Oh, yeah, the bus!

Despite the late hour, the high latitude of Alaska afforded us a few rays of late-night twilight to tour the bus and the surrounding area.

The bus, I was disappointed to see, was no

gleaming sanctum of holiness. It was a run-down, dilapidated rattletrap that would have looked in sorry shape even if it had been in the company of other junkyard jalopies. Like the perforated mouth of a jack o' lantern, twelve of the bus's twenty-six windows were missing, and the fourteen that remained were marked with the wounds of hurled rocks and rifle bullets. In the windowless gaps were tattered translucent plastic tarps, which someone must have slung up the summer before.

From the looks of all the trash piled around the bus, it seemed as if the bus had purged from its bowels a heap of detritus in its dying moments: crinkled cans of Miller Light, soggy tee shirts, moldy socks, bleached moose antlers, rusted oil drums, bottles of Carolina's Irish Cream, Makers 46 Bourbon, Monarch Gin. The place was a mess.

The ground was trampled dirt bearing only a few desperate sprouts of grass. A nearby fire pit was littered with warped configurations of burnt plastic. I went to search for fallen logs in the forest so we could build a fire, but all that was left were a few tiny twigs and a minefield of human feces and toilet paper.

Written on the driver-side body of the bus — the teal-colored backdrop where McCandless took the iconic photo of himself — were derisive poems, tic-tac-toe matches, and mocking graffiti like

"McCandless Resort and Casino." There were other messages like:

"We came, we saw, we sat and pondered, oh a life so silly, lost and squandered!"

"Memorial to dumbasses."

"It's easter and we're still alive you sucka."

The bus had clearly been bullied. Besides all the trash and shattered windows, parts of the bus were missing, like stuffing from the mattress Chris died on, and the instrument panel, which was sold for $177 on eBay.

I was amazed that people would come all this way to desecrate the site of someone else's death. At first, I thought that this was a sign that the potency of McCandless's story was finally fading; that people were ready to finally move on. But then I wondered if these scribblings were actually proof that the story still has staying power.

"Monuments are mortal," writes authors Robert S. Nelson and Margaret Rose Olin in their book, *Monuments and Memory, Made and Unmade*. "A monument often becomes so powerfully symbolic that someone acquires a vested interest in destroying it," they write. "This potential for destruction or defacement may be the most meaningful aspect of the monument's existence as an object." To aim to destroy a monument is to aim to destroy the symbol that the monument represents. It's a common tactic for those who want to erase history, ter-

rorists and governments alike. It's why the rigidly
theocratic Taliban destroyed Buddhist shrines in
Afghanistan. It's why a more egalitarian-minded
America wants to fold away the Confederate flag
and remove statues of Confederate generals. And
it's why the U.S. military infamously dragged a
statue of Saddam Hussein out of Firdos Square.
"But from such violence," writes Nelson and Olin,
"dreams and memories can emerge undamaged,
even strengthened." The deliberate desecration of
the bus, a symbol that represents McCandless's
story, is a sign, I thought, that the people who de-
spise his story still feel threatened by its symbols.

It's interesting to consider the history of the bus
and how it has changed symbolically. Its original
purpose on the Stampede was to transport work-
ers to an antimony mine in 1961. (The bus was not
actually driven but towed by a D-9 Caterpillar.)
When one of the bus's axles broke, the bus was
abandoned, and it thereafter served as a shelter
for traveling hunters and trappers. The bus, then,
represented development, industry, and practicality. And now that the bus has begun to represent
something else — spiritual fulfillment, romantic
adventure, spontaneous living — the champions
of practicality and industry wish to snuff out this
crazy free-spirited radicalism before the bus can
fan any more flames.

It's as if Chris's detractors worry that his story

will somehow encourage the nation's youth to callously abandon mothers and fathers and take off on death-defying jaunts into the wild, bringing down with them the feeble familial pillars that hold up society. But none of that will ever happen. Perhaps a few inspired extremists will get run over by freight trains, or catch malaria in the jungle, or starve in the wild. But just a few. Love for home and family and safety and security is too ingrained in our nature. But a select few — "the men ... cursed with the gypsy blood," as Robert Service put it — need something more than what conventional life offers.

Alfred Lansing, in his book, *The Endurance*, which chronicles Ernest Shackleton's ill-fated Antarctic expedition, offers insights into the explorer's mind. "Shackleton's unwillingness," Lansing writes, "to succumb to the demands of everyday life and his insatiable excitement with unrealistic ventures left him open to the accusation of being basically immature and irresponsible." The expedition to Antarctica, though, provided Shackleton with a task that was so enormous and demanding that it became "a touchstone for his monstrous ego and implacable drive."

Adventurers like Shackleton, Sir Edmund Hilary, and Robert Falcon Scott are perceived to have been romantic, bold, and daring, or — at worst — megalomaniacal and narcissistic. However,

McCandless — even though he, like the explorers, yearned to grapple with the grand — is written off as crazy or suicidal. In a 2006 essay, Peter Christian, a park ranger in Alaska, wrote what has become the quintessential and much-cited anti-McCandless essay in which he calls McCandless suicidal and mentally ill, and McCandless' journey, "stupid, tragic, and inconsiderate." If etched into the stone tablets of our genetic codes was the end goal of living the longest life possible, then Ranger Christian's diagnosis of McCandless might hold some truth. But McCandless, like the explorers of yore, lived by a different credo: Let us not live in fear of death but in fear of not having ever lived; to living full lives before long ones; to seizing the goddamned day.

And here is the dilemma of the modern-day explorer: They're afflicted with implacable drives, but there exists no grand, never-done-before-yet-somehow-practical endeavor to which they can apply that drive. And McCandless, born in an age when there were no new lands to discover and in a country where there were no "real" adventures to go on, had to, well, invent a journey of his own. And that's what's so enticing about McCandless's story. McCandless showed us that there are still twenty-first century adventures to embark on, still North American odysseys that need heroes and heroines. In the vocation-based, suck-it-up-and-get-a-job times we find ourselves in, McCandless gives the adventurous at heart, the modern-day nomads, the Shackletons of suburbia, an example of how we can live differently and create our own grand journeys. And that's the great service of travel books: When we juxtapose the author's or the subject's extreme dream with our comparatively modest but still outlandish dreams, we're empowered because the reading experience has broadened what we believe to be humanly possible.

Yet McCandless is derided by an enraged minority. For what? For following his dream? For momentarily leaving society? For trying out a new way of living? For dying? We have seven billion people on this planet. Shouldn't we goad on the few of us who are willing to go to the farthest reaches of the earth, their dreams, their human faculties? Shouldn't we embrace those few hardy souls who will walk through the gates of Hades, to the fringe of their physical limits, or unprepared into the Alaskan wild, so that — if by chance that they make it out alive — we'll have messengers who can report back and teach us something about what wonders and horrors exist outside the bubbles of our ordinary existences?

႟

I walked into the bus. The walls and ceiling were covered in names and dates that had overlapped one another several times. The windshield bore a network of cracks shaped like a spider web. There were two cots: one with a mattress that Chris died on, and the other, a bare skeleton of springs. To one side, in the middle of the bus, was a huge oil drum that served as a wood stove. There was a suitcase of books containing copies of *Into the Wild*, *The Bible*, *Alaska Trees and Wildflowers*, as well as Jack London's *Call of the Wild* and *White Fang*. A shelving unit held cans of soup, derelict hiking boots, binoculars, iso-butane canisters, a mosquito head net. With mud and debris and empty liquor bottles strewn across the floor, the place looked like an abandoned frat house the morning after a wild party. There was something eerie about the place. Except for the nearby Sushana River rippling in the background and a light breeze making the tattered window tarps quiver, the place was deathly still and quiet. I looked at the bed and could practically see the humps of McCandless's emaciated body withering away inside his sleeping bag. Dying because of a dream.

I imagined myself laying there — my younger self. I might have been thinking about how stupid I'd been to have made the mistakes I'd made, how sorry I was to have abandoned those I loved, and how nice it would be to be back in my parent's home, where I was positive I'd no longer be afflicted with romantic impulses and grandiose dreams. That's what I thought Chris might have been thinking, too.

I understood Chris. As a younger man, I was like Chris, though not nearly as extreme or audacious. Like him, I grew up in an uninspiring landscape of soccer fields and cookie cutter homes. And like him, I was completely uninterested with the prospect of the school/career/Winnebago/death formula that everyone else seemed okay with. I craved wild land and adventure with a passion that made people uncomfortable when I talked about my dream to drive to Alaska.

When I was twenty-one, between my fourth and fifth years of college, I — after years of postponement and cowardly reluctance — finally took off on a road trip to Alaska with a friend. To pay for the trip, we found jobs cleaning rooms at a truck stop sixty miles north of the Arctic Circle in a town of thirty-five people called Coldfoot, nestled in the heart of the Brooks Mountain Range. It was nowhere near the Stampede Trail, but it was similar in that it presented its inhabitants with a million doors through which they could enter the wilderness. On our first weekend off, my traveling companion and I, for the first time in our lives, walked through one of these doors — inadequately equipped, severely unprepared, and woefully inexperienced — and entered the wild.

It was the first hike of our lives, and our goal was a 5,900-foot mountain called Blue Cloud that was miles from any road and was within the boundaries of the Gates of the Arctic National Park. After a couple of hours, my friend turned back because of sore feet, leaving me alone in the mountains, where I'd trudge through unforgiving terrain, yell at boulders I thought were grizzlies, and flee from a group of Dall Sheep ewes who took only a passing interest in me, yet terrified me no less. I made it to the mountain, and then the peak, but got lost on my hike back to the road. I'd been walking without proper gear, little food, and hardly any water for twenty-eight hours straight. Because the sun hovered above the horizon for all hours of the night, I couldn't tell east from west. As I sat on a rock, helplessly gazing into the haze of an unchecked forest fire — unsure of in what direction I ought to head — I thought that this might be it for me. I thought that I might die out there. And in that moment, I wasn't thinking about the grandness of my adventure. I wasn't basking in a moment of nirvana, stirred up by this existential crisis. Instead, I just thought of my family and about how I had really screwed up.

In *Into the Wild*, author Jon Krakauer — to offer insights into Chris's motivations — spends two chapters discussing his near-death experiences climbing a mountain in Alaska called Devils Thumb when he was twenty-three. Krakauer made it to the peak and back home successfully, but he realized that, in the end, his climb changed nothing in his life. "I came to appreciate," Krakauer wrote, "that mountains make poor receptacles for dreams."

I, too, made it back from my hike, and like Krakauer, I didn't feel any sense of victory or exultation from accomplishing my goal. But unlike for him, everything had changed. I better understood to what lengths the human body and spirit could go. I was no longer as reserved, as weak-kneed, or as timid as I had been before. That journey, that foray into the wild, that summer in Alaska, had changed me. And while I was never again as reckless as I'd been when I decided to go on that trip, because of Blue Cloud I went on to spend my twenties living a reasonably adventurous life, going on two cross-country hitchhikes, canoeing across Canada for a summer, moving back up to Alaska to pay off my student debt, and living in a van for two years to get a graduate education, debt-free.

As I stood in the bus, looking at Chris's deathbed, I thought about how he might have come back home to live a still-adventurous-but-not-as-reckless life. Having scratched some of those adventurous itches, he might have gone on to strike a healthy balance between romanticism and practicality, between family duty and individualist ideals, between preserving his life and going to the wildest ends of the earth to seize the ever-fleeting sublime. Maybe he, like me, would go on a pilgrimage to see the site of another young man's death whose end came because of a fatal exuberance for life, where he might reflect on his own near-fatal and life-altering journeys as a younger man.

I slept in my tent beside the bus. Josh slept inside on Chris's bed, which I was too spooked to even touch. In the morning, I gave the bus another tour and leafed through a journal I found inside, into which over a hundred pilgrims had signed their names and shared their thoughts about McCandless and the bus.

Unlike those who desecrated the bus, these pilgrims came out here to honor the memory of Chris. I'd been affected by the squalor and haunted by the tragic events that took place there, but they didn't think of this bus as eerie or depressing; to them, this place was inspiring, blessed, and full of magic.

"The bus has a unique aura and has inspired so many people to change their way of life," wrote Max of Germany. "I think that's the greatest achievement and gift of Chris to the world. Thank you."

"I am blessed to be in a special place such as this," wrote Jay of Nova Scotia. "I feel just as blessed to have learned about you and your travels which have inspired me to love more, give more, and teach more to others. You were truly a gift to this world."

"Chris has inspired me," wrote Richard. "This trip is everything I wanted and more. There is a blessful feeling of peace in this magical bus."

"In absolute awe of the energy present," wrote Chris (not *the* Chris). "This is a very magic bus indeed. May we all bring it back and share it."

"Life has taken us here. Now we take life everywhere," wrote Joe, Mich, and Fab.

It was then — reading all these entries, looking at all the names etched into walls of the bus — that I realized that McCandless's story wasn't going away any time soon. As long as our society is structured in such a way that romantic longings are squelched, as long as young people are saddled with enormous student debts, as long as wild places are being seized from us and paved over by the captains of industry, we will seek stories of people who had the courage to find a way out. Until we find a way to harmonize our cities and neighborhoods and homes with nature, and until we think of the journey less as a way for unemployed slackers to postpone adulthood and more as a transformative stage of life, the Muirs and McCandlesses, the Ed Abbeys and Everett Ruesses, the Shackletons and Thoreaus — the extremists and explorers — will continue to titillate and tantalize.

The pilgrimage is a sort of simulation of the original journey. We pilgrims retrace the steps of the original journeyer, look over the same scenery, and hopefully have an experience that at least hints of the original journey, even if it's a secondary, watered-down sort of journey. We do it, perhaps, for simple tourism. Or, better yet, to commemorate the place or the people involved. If we cycle the Trail of Tears, we do it to honor, to pay our respects, and to get those around us to remember. But there's often something more to a pilgrimage than mere commemoration. We want something out of it—we want the special qualities of the person, place, or thing to rub off onto us, whether it be intellect, humor, bravery, athletic skill, musical talent, conviction. We re-walk the path of Selma's marchers to get a steroid shot of moral courage. We touch the Wailing Wall to fortify our religious beliefs, to fill ourselves with resilience. We go to Walden Pond hoping that we might soak up the atmosphere — the cool pond, the birdsong, the fecundity of a humid Massachusetts afternoon — and hope that the very atmosphere that flowed from earth and sky and pond into Thoreau's head, through his pen, and then onto page might flow through us, too. We want to be like these figures. We don't want to necessarily *be* them, but we want to gather and bring back a bit of their specialty, to be imbued with a hint of their one-of-a-kind worth.

Why was I here? What did I want out of the bus? If anything, it was Chris's ballsiness. His ability to turn a crazy idea into something real. I had the crazy ideas. That wasn't the problem. But the courage to follow through with them, to risk everything (and I'm talking about a career in letters here): that was something that was still, to me, an abstract concept.

cℑℑ

Josh and I took our photos seated in front of the bus, filled up our water bottles in the Soshana, packed up our stuff, and began our seventeen-mile haul back to civilization, where we were already looking forward to sumptuous feasts of Healy cuisine.

As I walked along the Stampede, shadowed by a canopy of birch and alder trees, I looked back at the bus one last time. I thought that while the story may continue to capture imaginations, I didn't think the bus would be there for much longer. I thought it would be great if it remained — or if it was even preserved — but I knew that there were too many people sickened by McCandless and his story. It wouldn't take much more than a match, a few canisters of gasoline, and a bottle of Canadian Crest to destroy the place. And if it isn't a renegade arsonist who puts an end to the bus, it could be local government, development interests, or even Mother Nature herself.

I thought that losing this place would be easier to stomach since the place had already lost its sense of purity; since the hide of wildness it once wore had been fleeced long ago. It was no longer wild, and as long as humankind persists, it probably never would be again. If it wasn't de-wilded by the book, the pilgrims, or the North Slope Militiamen who effortlessly drive their mud boggers through the Tek, it would be the tentacles of civilization that never cease to creep over our wild places. In 2004, for instance, the Park Service and Department of Natural Resources proposed plans to pave a ninety-mile road along the Stampede, where, at the site of the bus, there'd be a fee station, a developed campground, and a "defined parking area for automobiles, RVs and buses." Or, in another scenario, there'd be a maintained trail with a footbridge over the Tek and cabins by the bus. These proposals haven't passed and do not look like they will, but there's always the possibility of future development. (Between all out destruction and soul-killing bureaucratic preservation as possible fates for the bus, I'll vote for bureaucratic preservation, with all its interpretive signage, well-groomed trails, and ranger-led tours.)

If the wild isn't tamed by the tourism industry, it could be smoked out by gas interests, who currently have a lease to explore the Healy Basin for natural gas, including a large section of the Stampede, which gas companies may receive permission to frack. It's a sad irony of our times that the site of *Into the Wild* is becoming anything but wild.

But McCandless' story has little to do with this one place, or even wild places. The story is about self-transformation; about the power of a journey; about going on our own journeys to our own Magic Buses in whatever form they come.

On my journey back to civilization, standing before the Tek — which appeared slightly bigger and faster than it had been the day before — I thought about what it would be like to look at a river you knew couldn't be crossed.

But I was done thinking of McCandless. I had worries of my own to think about—worries about my farfetched dreams and whether I had the mettle to pursue them as aggressively as Chris might. My journey wasn't so much in ferocious landscapes anymore, but the "professional wilds," where the unknown seemed just as mountainous and mysterious and fraught with peril as the Brooks Range seemed to me years before. I had new types of

rivers to cross, but my doubts and insecurities —
like torrential downpours and glacial melt — had
turned mere trickles into feared Teklanikas.

Worried again about the possibility of getting
seized by the Tek, I plunged a leg into the water.
Looking at the opposite bank, I knew — whether
venturing into the wild or through the wilds of civilization — that the lesson to take back with me
was, when we come upon that which divides us
from our dreams, to cross. Unless death is certain,
cross. Yes, definitely cross.

Afterword:

The McCandless Mecca, Five Years Later

It is July 2018, and it has been seven years since I visited the bus and five since this tiny book published. Back in 2011, I pitched this story to a number of applicable magazines, including *Outside*, *Backpacker*, and Amazon's new Kindle Single platform. I was ignored or rejected by all, so I decided that I had no choice but to self-publish, and, five years later, I'm happy to declare this tiny book a tiny success. (If there was any benefit to the misfortune of having to self-publish, it was that I could write the book without having to observe a word count, and I'm glad this book got to stretch its legs to 10,000 words—well beyond what a traditional magazine would allow but an ideal sum, I think, to tell this story as best as it could be told.) It's sold around 2,800 copies and made me about $5,000, which is about the rate I would have gotten from one of those magazines.

It's not a bad sales report, but it's also pretty good for self-publishing standards.

My reason for a second edition of *The McCandless Mecca* is largely aesthetic. Back in 2013, I spent days designing my cover: a photo of my hiking boots in mid-step as I walk the Stampede Trail, overlaid with a carefully chosen font. I enjoyed the novelty of the process. I enjoyed flexing unused creative muscles. And I at one point thought it was actually good—borderline professional, even. It didn't take me long, though, to appreciate the truth. The cover looked amateurish (if passably amateurish), and I have since been bothered that this essay, of which I am proud, could have probably reached more eyes if it wasn't behind such a lousy cover.

I met a professional illustrator (Astrid Jaekel) who offered to update the cover. Plus, a friend in publishing (Acorn Abbey Books) offered to convert the ebook into a paperback, free of charge. So, for minimal effort, I realized I could enhance my product and maybe even give the book a second life in sales. *Into the Wild*, and the bus for that matter, haven't gotten any less popular in the last five years, so maybe this book will keep selling, too. It was an easy decision.

But there was more to it than aesthetic touch ups. I wanted to revisit this essay. I don't say this about my writing often, but I like this book. I always enjoy re-reading it. What I like about it is how much conviction there is in it. I'll think: this is a writer who has conviction and who isn't afraid to share it. It's not often enough that I can write so fearlessly about a subject. (I only have one other tiny book published these past five years.) But on the subject of McCandless, I felt clear-eyed. I felt like I understood the book and movie and McCandless in ways superior to most any other reader or viewer.

I began to lose this conviction in 2015, after I read Carine McCandless's *The Wild Truth*, which describes her and Chris's childhood. (Carine is Chris's sister.) It's brutal and devastating. The McCandless parents got off easy in the *Into the Wild* book and movie. (Carine explains that it's she, and not Krakauer, who's at fault for the initial inaccurate portrayals.) The McCandless kids grew up in an atmosphere of unrelenting abuse, chaos, and insanity. This was the sort of family in which the father made his children choose the belts they'd be beaten with.

The Wild Truth made me question Chris's primary motivation in heading to Alaska. Before *The Wild Truth*, I thought Chris was mainly a born wanderer who was destined to embark on an existential journey. But after *The Wild Truth* I felt as if, more than anything, Chris was running away from something.

Chris, as a literary figure, meant something to me because I identified with him, and I identified with him more than I identified with any other character in books or films. He, like me, was a disenchanted suburbanite who intuitively felt there was something seriously wrong with our surrounding, and seemingly inescapable, consumer-capitalist milieu. The search for something real and natural and untouched by the absurd surreality of the service economy was what drove us to Alaska, I thought. But now, after Carine's book, I thought that maybe he was primarily a victim of abuse, and since I had a nice family and a nice upbringing, I could no longer identify so much with him. It was as if I'd suddenly lost a kindred spirit. And I thought that maybe a lot of us lost someone in a way (except for people who had similar traumas and who might now feel a newfound kinship with him). After all, there are countless stories of people rebelling against terrible parents or overcoming hard childhoods, but there really aren't many recent stories of people rebelling against their culture and society. There really aren't that many modern-day Thoreaus or Jack Londons who can speak to those old values but in a more up-to-date and relevant sort of way. *Into the Wild* was that unique and relevant story, and I wondered if we all lost something special in learning the truth.

But will the truth prevail? It's 2018, four years

after Carine's book. When we think of Chris, do we think of Carine's Chris or Krakauer's Chris? We probably think of him as Kraukauer's Chris—a wanderer, an idealist, an adventurer. We haven't come to think of him as Carine has rightly depicted him, and it may be unlikely that we ever will. Humanity craves symbols, legends, mythic figures, and we will discard reality if it gets in the way of our precious stories and precious heroes. And I think our present society craves — *needs* — McCandless to be the youthful adventurer, so much that we will collectively plug our ears to the truth and remember what we want to remember.

I don't know where I stand on the issue. The truth, in almost all cases, is preferable, and Carine's efforts appear to be genuine and well-meant (and I get the feeling that her book is entirely truthful). But at the same time I wonder: Why not let us remember him how we want to remember him? Given how continually popular his story is, it's clearly serving some useful social purpose. I wonder if the truth could rob us of something far more valuable than the truth?

In the end, it's out of our hands. Dealing with something as amorphous as the "collective memory" is next to impossible. The world will remember Chris as it wants to: a passionate adventurer to some, a naive fool to others. Others may remember him as a tortured soul, whose sole motivation was to flee, and not to seek.

To be honest, I don't know if I can even remember him differently from Krakauer's Chris, even though I'm acquainted with the truth of things. My memory of him — as idealistic adventurer — has landed like an anchor in my brain. It's half-lodged in the ocean bed with a rusty, bisected chain coiled around it. It's not going anywhere soon.

And apparently the bus isn't going anywhere, neither. Since the publication of this tiny book, the bus is still a popular pilgrimage destination. I did a quick Google search and there appears to be a steady train of pilgrims, several of whom, every summer, require search and rescues. I think this will probably go on for years to come, until something truly terrible happens. A mass drowning of pilgrims trying to cross the Tek? A lethal confrontation with ornery locals? Or maybe the bus will get dismembered or beaten to a pulp? One of these outcomes seems inevitable, and it's for that reason that I think the bus should be preserved and made into a proper monument or a state park site. Many would-be pilgrims will bemoan the fact that they didn't get the same opportunity to visit the bus in its natural state (and I'll be forever grateful to have had the chance to see the bus in its historic environs), but I'd only argue that tacky preservation is better than nothing all at.

Or maybe it doesn't matter if the bus is there or not. Chris lived and died in that special spot near the Soshana, and no one is capable of removing a section of the earth, so there will always be a set of coordinates leading to a place, where, bus or no bus, we can commemorate Chris and maybe gather a bit of his ballsiness.

As for me, I ended up making the most of my Alaskan summer. I went on a lot of hikes (several with Josh), got a girlfriend, and even made a little side money working at Coldfoot. Mostly, I worked on my first book, *Walden on Wheels*, which got published, as have two more in subsequent years. My writing career is checkered and financially shaky. (I'm trying to milk this five-year-old book for a few more bucks, so it should be clear to you that I'm not getting rich off of my words.) But, ultimately, writing has been a success, and I attribute a lot of that to my wilderness adventures. Going on a trip on your own in the wilderness and coming back alive has certainly helped with confidence, self-esteem, and even humility. Saying you're going to be an author — and then making it happen — takes some gutsiness, and gutsiness, I've learned, is as much an innate quality as it is a muscle that must be built, flexed, and maintained. In this way, there's little difference between climbing a mountain and writing a book proposal. In the end, they both require believing in the absurd delusions, *Yes, I can do it* & *No, I'm not going to give up.* If there'd been no such thing as wilderness, I might today lack the requisite wildness (or gutsiness, whatever you want to call it) to do what I've done.

I hiked to the Magic Bus with youthful exuberance and I wrote this tiny book, as you've probably noted, with youthful exuberance. And I write this afterword, at age 35, feeling like I'm more or less the same guy I was back then. There was once a time, perhaps in my very early twenties, when I felt unstoppable, as if there was no such thing as an uncrossable river. And there will be a time when I'll know for sure which rivers aren't to be crossed. Both approaches have their advantages: the younger can brashly, stupidly, accidentally do the undoable; the older isn't going to unwisely take any too-dumb risks. Until then, I happily abide in that sweet spot where youthful heedlessness and wisdom-driven conservatism vie, where goals and dreams are more measured but where there's still the occasional calling for the grand, the bold, the undoable.

And it's for this reason why I'm happy to return to this book: it speaks to a constancy of character; it reminds me of where I've come from and who I am, or at least who I can be when I'm better than my worst. It reminds me to keep writing, to keep taking chances, and to keep wilderness in my life.

I don't know who the real Chris McCandless is and what he might say. What's the one message he'd like to deliver? Would he like *Into the Wild*? Would he like *The McCandless Mecca*, or would he tell me I've gotten it all wrong? I thought I knew Chris, but maybe I don't. Maybe it doesn't matter, because when it comes to the stories we love, what ultimately matters is what helps us more than what's true, so long as what helps us is true.

Acknowledgments

I'd like to thank Josh Spice, not only for visually documenting our journey, but also for outfitting us with gear and driving us to the Stampede. I'd like to thank Astrid Jaekel (www.astridjaekel.com) for the cover design. And I'd also like to thank David Dalton of Acorn Abbey Books (www.acornabbey.com/publishing) for preparing the paperback for print. These are all close friends, who've offered their help to me without seeking any compensation in return. I count myself lucky to have such generous, supportive friends.

About the author

Ken Ilgunas is an author, journalist, and backcountry ranger in Alaska. He has hitchhiked ten thousand miles across North America, paddled one thousand miles across Ontario in a birchbark canoe, and walked 1,700 miles across the Great Plains, following the proposed route of the Keystone XL pipeline. The author of *Walden on Wheels*, *Trespassing Across America*, and *This Land Is Our Land*, he is from Wheatfield, New York.

About the photographer

Josh Spice lives in Eugene, Oregon. His work can be found on staysanesleepoutside.com.

Made in the USA
Monee, IL
18 August 2022

11947472R10046